MW00657334

1441 Sixth Avenue
San Diego, CA 92101

AMAZING WOMEN

AMAZING WOMEN
Amazing World

MARSH ENGLE

JODERE
GROUP
SAN DIEGO, CALIFORNIA

Published by Jodere Group, Inc.
P.O. Box 910147, San Diego, CA 92191-0147
(800) 569-1002 • www.jodere.com

Cover Photo: Zina Bethune and Sarah Anderson from Bethune Theatredanse.
Photographer: Lancelot Kettler, © Bethune Theatredanse

Book design: Steven Guddat

CIP data available from the Library of Congress

ISBN 1-58872-030-6

04 03 02 01 4 3 2 1
1st printing, February 2002

Printed in Canada

A journey of a thousand miles
must begin with a single step.

- Chinese proverb

This book is dedicated to my amazing Mother, Evelyn Louise Henry.
You helped me with so very many of my first steps! You are love.

And, to every woman in the world.
May you always recognize and honor
the amazing woman who lives inside of you.
Express, dream and create
through love, with love, in love, always.

Marsh Engle

Introduction

Throughout my life I have been deeply touched and deeply impressed by the power of women. My experience has been that it is a quiet power, not a blustery one; a true power, not a false one; a kind power, not a cruel one. It is, in a word, the power of love.

My own greatest living example of this is Nancy Fleming-Walsch, my wife. She is the most powerful woman I know.

Nancy's power is very quiet. A gentle woman, she rarely raises her voice, never pontificates, has absolutely no need to boast, does not understand what it means to swagger, yet moves into a room with a soft peace that brings more power to the space than all my swaggering and boasting and pontificating combined.

Nancy's power is very true. True power rarely has to be revealed, and is virtually never fully exercised. It simply is, and that is sufficient. This is my experience of Nancy. She does not find it necessary to express power as an exertion of control, but, rather, experiences power as a lack of the need to control. By moving easily with the flow of life, she harnesses the power of life itself. Rather than pushing against it, she merges with it. This makes her easy in the moment (whatever the moment is bringing), and strong in the current (wherever the current is taking us). I have relied on this power more than once in our life together, and always it has taken me to safe harbor.

Nancy's power is very kind. She believes in power with, not power over. Her idea of being full of power is having sufficient power to fill another. She has demonstrated this to me in a hundred ways over a thousand days across a million moments in our lives. Always supporting me in whatever I have undertaken, she has been, in truth and in fact, the wind beneath my wings. When I have been weak and discouraged, she has given me strength and courage. When I have been saddened and fearful, she has returned me to my vision. When I have been sick, she has comforted me. When I have been lonely, she has companioned me. When I have been thirsty for love, she has poured the gentleness of her heart into my soul.

Her intuitions are infallible, her advice invariably sound, her help always present, always offered, and always, in the end, crucial to the outcome. I am amazed at her resourcefulness, blessed by her patience, profited by her insights, and stunned by her emotional generosity. What I try to overwhelm, she tries to overlook. When I am prepared to complain, she is prepared to compliment. When I give in to a scowl, she gives in to a smile. When I seek to reprimand, she seeks to repair.

Whether with hotel front-desk clerks or airline counter ticket agents, late-arriving telephone repairmen, or employees of firms with whom we are doing business, she is always quick to grant the benefit of the doubt, forgive and forget, and extend a word of kindness.

Nancy moves through the world with a special grace.

Like all amazing women, she has touched and taught in profound and important ways those with whom she has shared her life. And yet, as wonderful as Nancy Fleming-Walsch is, she is by no means unique. Sometimes I think that God has bestowed a special gift on women. So many of them are utterly amazing and powerful and I have been profoundly blessed to know, personally, more than a few.

You have a chance to come to know a few more right now, for you are holding in your hand a collection of remarkable stories about women. As you read these stories, you will learn not only about these women in particular, but about the qualities and the attributes of all amazing women, many of whom are no doubt touching your own life even in this day and time.

I hope, then, that these stories will awaken your consciousness, enlarge your awareness, and attune you to what is true about, and what is going on in, the world around you. And especially, the women in your life. They are one half of the world's greatest resource – its people. And most of the world has not honored them in that way.

Let us, then, begin.

Let us learn about....Amazing Women.

Neale Donald Walsch, author
Conversations with God

About the women in this book . . .

Nearly three years ago I set out on a quest to explore the inner spirit of the amazing woman. I wanted to feel and experience her world - learn of her capacity to shift resistance to strength, fear to courage and how she takes action with intent and purpose. What I learned from the women I discovered along my journey profoundly transformed my life.

The women in this book are a glimmering expression of love, gratitude and acceptance. Unforgettable women, they embrace life, loving and loss fully and boldly. They dream big and listen deeply. May their words and stories serve as powerful reflections of your own possibilities. Celebrate and enjoy!

Marsh Engle

Action

"The next time you find yourself feeling afraid, tell yourself, 'I am strong, I am courageous – I have wisdom.' These are the three most powerful words of action. Once you embrace these words in your everyday life, taking action is simple."

Kathleen Baty

Advocate for Victim Rights, Personal Safety Expert

Kathleen Baty knows what it is to be afraid.

Twenty years ago Kathleen received a phone call that would change her life forever. In that instant, her caller, a high school acquaintance, became her stalker. After dozens of arrests and broken restraining orders he captured Kathleen in her own home. She was held hostage at knifepoint during a terrifying 11-hour standoff with police.

Kathleen Baty decided to fight back. As a journalist and reporter, she chose to shift the energy she had invested in fear into empowering herself and audiences across the nation. It was her dedication to victims' rights that helped to establish our country's first federal anti-stalking legislation, signed into law by President Clinton in August 1998.

Kathleen Baty is a woman of action – action that helps to ensure the safety of women everywhere.

Beauty

"Simply by looking into her spirit, I can see beauty in every woman!"

Vera Brown
Humanitarian and Founder of Vera Brown Cosmetics

Beauty

Vera Brown is an angel of beauty to hundreds – reaching out to the homeless, to the blind and to young women with a history of abuse. She sees the splendor of their spirit and helps them to rebuild and restore their confidence and self-esteem.

As a beautiful young woman raising her young son in Jamaica, Carol was successfully running her own hardware store when her ordeal began. Two men entered her store, tied her down and poured battery acid over her face and left her to die. But Carol was determined to live.

When Vera met Carol Guscott, she learned that the acid had destroyed more than Carol's face and eyes. She had lost the business that she had built to escape the poverty she was born to in Jamaica. Her friends fled, too horrified to look at the blistered flesh that was once a face. Her mother ran from her daughter's hospital room crying, "That's not my Carol." Her son fainted when he saw what his mother had become. Her fiancé, the man she had always dreamed of meeting, left for good.

But, what Vera saw radiating beyond the scars was the spirit of a beautiful woman.

Vera moved into action to help. She encouraged Carol to accompany her to the Foundation for the Junior Blind, where Carol soon became a popular friend. Vera recognized that this would be a safe and nurturing environment where Carol would find acceptance. This would become the place where Carol Guscott would begin to rebuild and restore.

"We are constantly rebuilding, renewing, restoring."

Carol Guscott

Choice

"I think a lot of people are afraid and don't realize that they're able to make choices. Make a choice! If it turns out to be wrong, make another. Remember, choices are unlimited. It's your life, so enjoy!"

Kathy Buckley
Acclaimed Hearing-Impaired Comedienne

Kathy Buckley grew up in a silent world. Born with a hearing loss that went undetected until she was eight, her family and teachers assumed she was slow. She experienced sexual abuse, was run over by a jeep, and stricken with cancer all before the age of thirty. Rather than be overcome with despair, Kathy chose to reach out through laughter.

Kathy Buckley is a woman who made a powerful choice: to overcome all the challenges life sent her way and to bravely meet them with dignity and laughter.

When Candace Sandy and Dawn Marie Daniels decided to write a book, neither woman recognized what their creative endeavor would reveal. Friends since high school, their mission was to compile a powerful book filled with the stories of lessons learned and wisdom gained by black women across America. What they experienced was their own personal transformation, as well as the transformation of the women who contributed to the book and the thousands of women they met in their travels.

"The writing of this book helped us heal things in ourselves that we didn't realize needed healing."

Their book, *Souls of My Sisters*, communicates the healing stories of their journey and gives women the opportunity to gain strength, acceptance, love, and camaraderie through shared experiences.

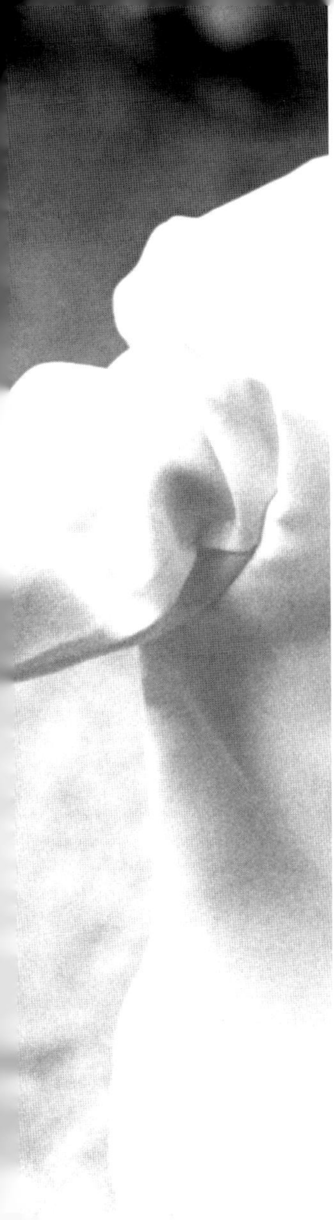

Communication

"Writing our book helped us to put the responsibility for healing in our own hands, the hands of the women who were brave enough to share their stories in the book and anyone who picked up the book to read the stories of faith and triumph. Through the process we realized that we, as black women, have suppressed and hidden our pain in order to survive, but now it's time to share and to heal. By collecting and reading other black women's stories, we were able to access communication buried deep within and share that communication with all of our sisters."

Candace Sandy
Dawn Marie Daniels
Authors of Souls of My Sisters

Compassion

"The men we lost that day were the bravest people you could ever imagine. In the 19 years I've been a New York City Firefighter, my mission has never been clearer than it is right now – my purpose is to help my firehouse heal."

Rochelle "Rocky" Jones
Captain, Engine 4, Fire Department of the City of New York

Rocky Jones knows bravery. She knows strength and courage. And Rocky Jones knows that God has given her a mission. On September 11, 2001, fourteen men from the firehouse she captains were lost during rescue attempts at the World Trade Center. Her firehouse was the second unit to respond to the call. When the men of her unit were called into action, Rocky was away on vacation. The man who was covering for her remains missing.

Since the day of the tragedy, Rocky has acted as a nurturing spirit to help the men of her unit heal from the loss, a role she embraces with love and compassion. Rocky Jones is one of only 25 women among 11,800 firefighters working for the Fire Department of the City of New York. Coming from a family of firefighters, she's carved her way through the ranks and was among the first women to be accepted to the department in 1982.

Confidence

"As a little girl I remember dreaming of a day that I would be on television. At times that dream felt so big. What I know today is that if we commit to our dream with confidence in our abilities and take action with an absolute belief in the possibilities, *anything* is possible!"

Ana Maria Montero
Anchor – Correspondent, CNN en Español

Today Ana Maria Montero is living her dream. In 1997, she became one of the youngest CNN en Español correspondents ever. She's covered Hollywood events including the Emmys, Grammys and Oscars, and she's interviewed top artists including Julia Roberts, Brad Pitt, Penelope Cruz and Nicholas Cage.

Dignity

"The worst secret is the one everyone around you knows but never talks about."

Meg Clairmonte
Subject and Co-Author of *Ultimate Judgment*
Ultimate Judgment: A Story of Emotional Corruption, Obsession and Betrayal, by Meg Clairmonte and Aurora Mackey, Health Communications, Inc., ©Feburary 2001

With these haunting words, Meg Clairmonte stepped forward to reclaim her life. No longer would she remain the powerless little girl told to keep forever quiet. Nor would she continue to endure the silent suffering that had lasted for nearly three decades. She would conceal the secrets no longer. Meg would fight for her dignity.

Meg's childhood sexual abuse at the hands of her millionaire stepfather lasted into adulthood. Years after he died, she chose to fight the ghosts of her past in a courtroom. An act that would require her to bravely face down her own mother who had conspired for years to ensure her daughter's passivity and silence. Her courageous battle became a precedent-setting legal case.

Meg Clairmonte regained her dignity. In doing so, she offered comfort and justice to scores of women who have suffered from sexual abuse.

Esteem

"As the only brown-skinned girl in an all-white New Jersey middle school, I grew up wanting to be what I could not be – to the point of hating who I was. As a model, I again found myself fighting against the limited opportunities – being seen as either too exotic or not exotic enough. From the encounters of my early life experience sprung my passion to revolutionize the beauty ideal."

Lubna Khalid
Founder of Real Cosmetics, Color for Women of Color

After spending seven years as a Pakistani-American fashion model in the U.S. and abroad, Lubna founded Real Cosmetics. Her vision: revolutionize the beauty ideal, creating new role models that reflect and celebrate the richness of their cultures and traditions. Real Cosmetics fulfills the cosmetic needs of all women of color: Latina, South Asian, East Asian, Middle Eastern, Black/African American, Native American and multi-ethnic women.

Expression

"Sarah is ten. She has osteogenesis. Her bones aren't strong enough to carry her body . . . but her heart is full enough to DANCE! Creativity shouldn't be cut off just because of a limitation. A disability doesn't diminish the need to share JOY or feel BEAUTY. It just means ACHIEVING that self-expression and communication in a different way."

Zina Bethune
Pioneer in the area of dance
for mentally and physically challenged children

With the help of Zina Bethune, mentally and physically challenged children have found their own creativity and self-worth through the beautiful art of dance. As Artistic Director of Bethune Theatredanse, through her Dance Outreach program for disabled children to learn and perform dance, she remains dedicated to the ideal that "art transcends limitations, creating its own rich being."

Images: Zina Bethune and Sarah Anderson from Bethune Theatredanse, Photographer: Lancelot Kettler, © Bethune Theatredanse

Faith

"We need love and faith to have the power to help humanity in its difficulties. In my long life of 92 years, I have held a great communication with God. All anyone needs in order to create beautiful miracles is to simply be in communication with God. God is that place of love and faith that lives within you."

Mother Sarita
Mother of don Miguel Ruiz, author of The Four Agreements

Faith and love live in you.

Mother Sarita is a beautiful living legacy who has achieved healings beyond the realm of traditional medicine for four decades. Sarita has said that it is not her own personal power that does the healing, it is her faith and the faith of others that creates these miracles. Sarita is the mother of don Miguel Ruiz and was his first Toltec teacher.

Healing

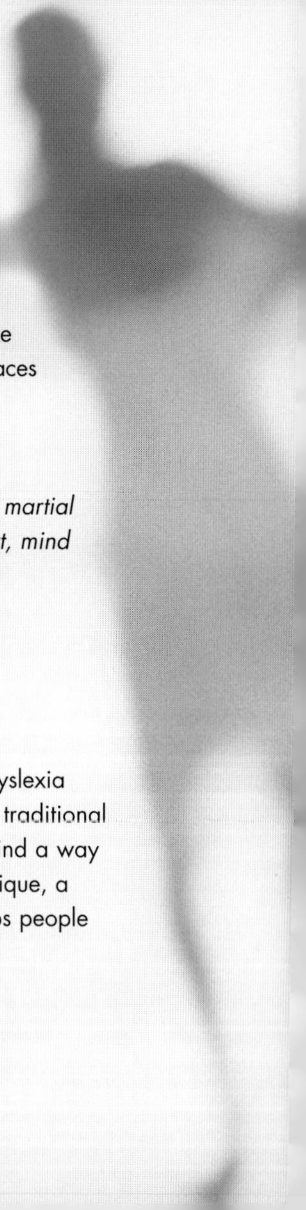

"A woman's body and spirit is the giver, the one who knows how to embrace and receive, how to hold close and nurture. The power to speak my voice, to take action, to create from the path of my heart is what I do as a woman who embraces her power. I believe life is meant to be passionate, sexy, alive and joyful."

Debbie Rosas
Founder of the Nia Technique, a unique and imaginative blend of dance and martial arts movements that engages the individual spirit while strengthening the heart, mind and emotional self.

Through movement we heal.

As a young girl, Debbie Rosas grew up with the feeling that she was stupid. Dyslexia and a debilitating lisp left her with deep frustration as she tried to fit into the traditional model of learning. This early childhood experience would spark a search to find a way to fully heal, a way of expression, and ultimately the creation of the Nia Technique, a mind, body, and spirit fitness modality recognized worldwide as one that helps people discover more about themselves, healing and movement.

Joy

"Live in your abundance. Give it to yourself. It is here you will find your greatest joy."

Debra Wilson
Television Star of MadTV, Humanitarian, Motivational Speaker

Joy

Through her own personal journey, Debra Wilson is a woman who is learning deeply and gaining immensely. Today, she is ready to respond to the needs of all people as a powerful woman who embraces her life with consciousness, love and gratitude.

"The lessons of my life are powerful gifts from God.
I honor each as a catalyst to help me share love and joy with the world."

Debra is committed to using the wisdom she's gained from her own life to touch the lives of others. Reaching out to offer words of encouragement to students of all ages with a special concern for "at-risk" and "high-risk" youth, she's determined to help them recognize their own magnificence – the place where they will discover their greatest joy.

Purpose

"I passionately believe
that the answer to
many of the world's problems
is to help children become
'agents of peace'
in their own schools,
neighborhoods, and communities.
Only then can we hope to stop
the insidious cycle
that rips apart families, cities,
and nations."

Kathy Eldon
Television Producer,
Author, Inspirer

Purpose

It was a tragedy of breathtaking scale – a young life cut short – that led Kathy to the discovery of a life of purpose. In 1993, her son, 22-year-old photojournalist Dan Eldon, was killed in Somalia while covering the famine and civil war. He was stoned to death by a mob of the very people he was trying to help. It was an unthinkable act of violence; a tragedy that robbed the world of a remarkable young man who filled his world with travel, photography, charitable expeditions, and hope.

Now, thanks to the love of his mother, Dan's dream to bring solutions to the world would not end in the violent streets of Somalia. Her Emmy-nominated documentary, *Dying to Tell the Story,* that she executive produced and her daughter Amy presented, is one that is now shown in schools of journalism and photography around the world. Their CNN documentary profiling the Colombian Children's Peace Movement (twice nominated for the Nobel Peace Prize) premiered at the United Nations and is being distributed by UNICEF. Their latest production, *Global Trek*, a new PBS series, inspires young people to be more aware of, and involved in, the world around them and helps to introduce people with solutions that contribute to solving some of the world's biggest challenges.

Spirit

"I believe every individual has personal mountains to climb and that anything can be achieved with an indomitable spirit, belief in a dream, and a desire to dare."

Laura Evans
Founder of Expedition Inspiration

"Twelve days, 11 hours, and 40 minutes after we had begun this journey to the peak of Argentina's Mt. Aconcagua, we were truly on top of the world. I brushed the tears from my eyes for those who would not share in the glory of the moment and willed my energy and hope to the millions of women who needed it... This was the only way I would have wanted to celebrate the five-year anniversary of my cancer diagnosis."

For Laura Evans this climb had been a miraculous journey from the edge of death to the victory of a lifetime – she had beat the odds and won her battle with breast cancer. With the triumph of Aconcagua, Laura and her team were able to send a powerful message of hope and determination to women everywhere.

In her memory: Laura Steele Evans, founder of Expedition Inspiration Fund for Breast Cancer, who was an inspiration to thousands of people with a life-threatening illness, passed away on October 17, 2000 of a brain tumor. May we always remember the love and hope she shared.

In Gratitude

Our entire life is simply a journey filled with a continuum of experiences that lead us to the perfect moment for a new awareness to be revealed. Some of these experiences are powerful and life changing. All are immensely important to our quest.

For me, getting to this moment has truly been a magical continuum of lessons. Every single one has been perfect for the new insight it delivered to me about myself. I give thanks to the Universe for allowing those awakenings. May I forever embrace my life with love and authenticity.

Thank you Mom and Dad, you were the perfect mirrors of love and inspiration. To my sons, Jason and Jon, who always believed even when I had a "moment" of doubt. To my family, for your love and support.

Thank you Jeff d'Avanzo, your strength and unwavering intent held us steady. To my agent, Bonnie Solow for knowing it would be. To my publisher, Debbie Luican, for seeing the vision and sharing the love of this message.

Bev Oswald, Mike Frierdich, John Steinhauer, Gail Stone and Susan Sheller for hanging in there through the early days. Dana Escalante for asking me the question that urged me forward. Ardice Faoro for her honesty. Gene Khoury for his total faith. Eddie Conner for helping to reveal my path long before I could see it. Noah Carson for the enlightened messenger he is. Don Miguel Ruiz for his powerful teachings. Rita Rivera for providing me an assured bridge to find my way. Uzma Khalid for helping me to recognize my true intent. Gaya Jenkins for moving me closer to my truth. Carol Toone for your love.

Thanks Loren Slocum, Cynthia Brian, Katherine Martin for the encouragement you share. To Vera Brown, Kathy Eldon, Kathleen Baty, Kathy Buckley, Debbie Rosas, Meg Clairmonte, Debra Wilson and all of the women I met along my journey of writing this book. Wow, did I ever learn from you! You are all AMAZING WOMEN!

With love and gratitude - Marsh Engle

About the Author . . .

Marsh Engle champions the expedition of personal awareness, transformation and inspiration. After many years of work as a marketing consultant and producer for the entertainment industry, in 1999 she shifted her attention exclusively to the creation of projects that inspire action in the lives of people.

She's explored a range of sacred beliefs and practices, documented spiritual vision quests to sacred sites for television and magazines, and established an annual, nationwide day to inspire love and confidence among women.

Marsh Engle lives in Los Angeles, California.

To learn more about Amazing Women visit
www.AmazingWomen.org

We hope you enjoyed this Jodere Group book.
If you would like additional information
about Jodere Group, Inc., please contact:

JODERE
GROUP

P.O. Box 910147 San Diego, CA 92191-0147
(800) 569-1002 www.jodere.com